BEHIND THE CURTAIN
Act Out History's BIGGEST Dramas

CITIZENS IMPRISONED

JAPANESE INTERNMENT CAMPS

Virginia Loh-Hagan

45TH PARALLEL PRESS

Published in the United States of America by Cherry Lake Publishing
Ann Arbor, Michigan
www.cherrylakepublishing.com

Reading Adviser: Marla Conn, MS, Ed., Literacy specialist, Read-Ability Inc.
Cover Designer: Felicia Macheske

Photo Credits: © Prazis Images/Shutterstock.com, cover, 1; © Library of Congress, LC-USW33-038539-ZC, 5; © Library of Congress, LC-DIG-hec-47188, 6; © Library of Congress, LC-USZ62-34565, 9; © Library of Congress, LC-USZ62-16555, 11; © Library of Congress, LC-USZ62-23602, 12; © Library of Congress, LC-USF346-081814-E, 17; © Library of Congress, LC-USZ62-137821, 18; © Library of Congress, LC-DIG-ppprs-00348, 21; © Library of Congress, LC-DIG-ppprs-00250, 22; © Library of Congress, LC-DIG-ppprs-00354, 25, © Library of Congress, LC-DIG-ppprs-00369, 29

Graphic Elements Throughout: © Chipmunk131/Shutterstock.com; © Nowik Sylwia/Shutterstock.com; © Andrey_Popov/Shutterstock.com; © NadzeyaShanchuk/Shutterstock.com; © KathyGold/Shutterstock.com; © Black creator/Shutterstock.com; © Edvard Molnar/Shutterstock.com; © Elenadesign/Shutterstock.com; © estherpoon/Shutterstock.com

45th Parallel Press is an imprint of Cherry Lake Publishing.

Library of Congress Cataloging-in-Publication Data

Names: Loh-Hagan, Virginia, author.
Title: Citizens imprisoned : Japanese internment camps / Virginia Loh-Hagan.
Description: Ann Arbor, Michigan : Cherry Lake Publishing, [2020] | Series: Behind the curtain | Includes index.
Identifiers: LCCN 2019032922 (print) | LCCN 2019032923 (ebook) | ISBN 9781534159419 (hardcover) | ISBN 9781534161719 (paperback) | ISBN 9781534160569 (pdf) | ISBN 9781534162860 (ebook)
Subjects: LCSH: Japanese Americans–Evacuation and relocation, 1942-1945–Juvenile literature. | World War, 1939-1945–Japanese Americans–Juvenile literature.
Classification: LCC D769.8.A6 L64 2020 (print) | LCC D769.8.A6 (ebook) | DDC 940.53/1773–dc23
LC record available at https://lccn.loc.gov/2019032922
LC ebook record available at https://lccn.loc.gov/2019032923

Cherry Lake Publishing would like to acknowledge the work of the Partnership for 21st Century Learning, a Network of Battelle for Kids. Please visit *http://www.battelleforkids.org/networks/p21* for more information.

Printed in the United States of America
Corporate Graphics

A Note on Dramatic Retellings

Participating in Readers Theater, or dramatic retellings, can greatly improve reading skills, especially fluency. The books in the **BEHIND THE CURTAIN** series give readers opportunities to learn about important historical events in a fun and engaging way. These books serve as a bridge to more complex texts. All the characters are real figures from history; however, their stories have been fictionalized. To learn more about the people and the events, check out the Viewpoints and Perspectives series and the Perspectives Library series, as the **BEHIND THE CURTAIN** books are aligned to these stories.

TABLE of CONTENTS

HISTORICAL BACKGROUND 4

CAST OF CHARACTERS 8

ACT 1 10

ACT 2 20

EVENT TIMELINE 30

Consider This! 31

Learn More 31

Index 32

About the Author 32

HISTORICAL BACKGROUND

Sunday, December 7, 1941, is a day to remember. Japan attacked Pearl Harbor. Pearl Harbor is a navy base in Hawaii. This took the United States by surprise. The next day, the United States declared war on Japan. It entered World War II.

Some Americans thought that Japanese Americans were spies. There was no proof of this. But the country gave in to the fear. President Franklin D. Roosevelt signed **Executive Order** 9066. He did this in 1942. The law forced Japanese Americans into **internment** camps. This happened from 1942 to 1945. It affected about 117,000 Japanese Americans.

The War **Relocation Authority** (WRA) was set up. It was in charge of moving the Japanese Americans.

FLASH FACT!

Japanese planes led the attack on Pearl Harbor.

Vocabulary

executive order (ig-ZEK-yuh-tiv OR-dur) a law issued by the president

internment (in-TURN-muhnt) the state of being confined like a prisoner

relocation (ree-loh-KAY-shuhn) moving from one place to another

authority (uh-THOR-ih-tee) being in charge

FLASH FACT!

President Franklin D. Roosevelt spoke to Congress to declare war.

Vocabulary

remote (rih-MOHT)
far away from cities

barbed (BAHRBD)
having hooks or spikes

Japanese Americans were taken from their homes. They took only what they could carry. They were sent to centers near their homes. From there, they were taken to camps. They lived at the camps until the war ended.

The camps were in remote areas. Some camps were at fairgrounds or racetracks. People lived where animals were kept. They created their own towns. They built houses. They built schools. They built hospitals. They built gardens. They did this with very little money and supplies.

Guard towers and barbed wire surrounded the camps. People who tried to escape were shot. The camps were like jails.

CAST of CHARACTERS

NARRATOR: person who helps tell the story

HELEN WATANABE: a fourth-grade Japanese American girl interned at Manzanar

MRS. WATANABE: mother of Helen

SOLDIER: someone who works in the U.S. Army whose job is to relocate Japanese Americans

MAS YUBU: an 18-year-old Japanese American soldier who is interned at Manzanar

GRACE JONES: a white teacher whose first job is teaching at Manzanar

GUARD: someone who works at Manzanar whose job is to protect or control

BACKSTORY
SPOTLIGHT BIOGRAPHY

Jeanne Wakatsuki Houston was born in 1934. She was born in Inglewood, California. She's the youngest of 10 children. She's Japanese American. She's a writer. Her most famous book is *Farewell to Manzanar*. She shared her own true story. She was forced into an internment camp at age 7. She and her family were taken to Manzanar. She lived at the camp for 3 years. Life was tough. Her big family had to live in a small space. They had very little. They were treated unfairly. But they survived. Her story was made into a TV movie. The book and movie are taught in many schools. Houston said she wants to keep telling others her story because she doesn't want history to repeat itself.

FLASH FACT!

Japanese Americans faced prejudice and discrimination after the attack on Pearl Harbor.

ACT 1

NARRATOR: *It's December 7, 1941.* **HELEN WATANABE** *is with her mother* **MRS. WATANABE** *in Los Angeles, California.*

MRS. WATANABE: Be quiet! Listen to the radio. Did you hear that?

HELEN: Japan attacked Pearl Harbor.

MRS. WATANABE: Oh no! That's not good for us.

HELEN: Pearl Harbor is in Hawaii. That's far away. We should be safe.

MRS. WATANABE: Our lives will never be the same again. We're Japanese. We'll get blamed for this.

HELEN: That doesn't make sense. You've lived in California for over 20 years. I was born here. We're Americans. We're **loyal**.

MRS. WATANABE: It doesn't matter. We look different. People will fear us. They'll think we're the enemies. They'll think we work for Japan.

HELEN: Oh, Mother! That can't be true. All will be well. You'll see.

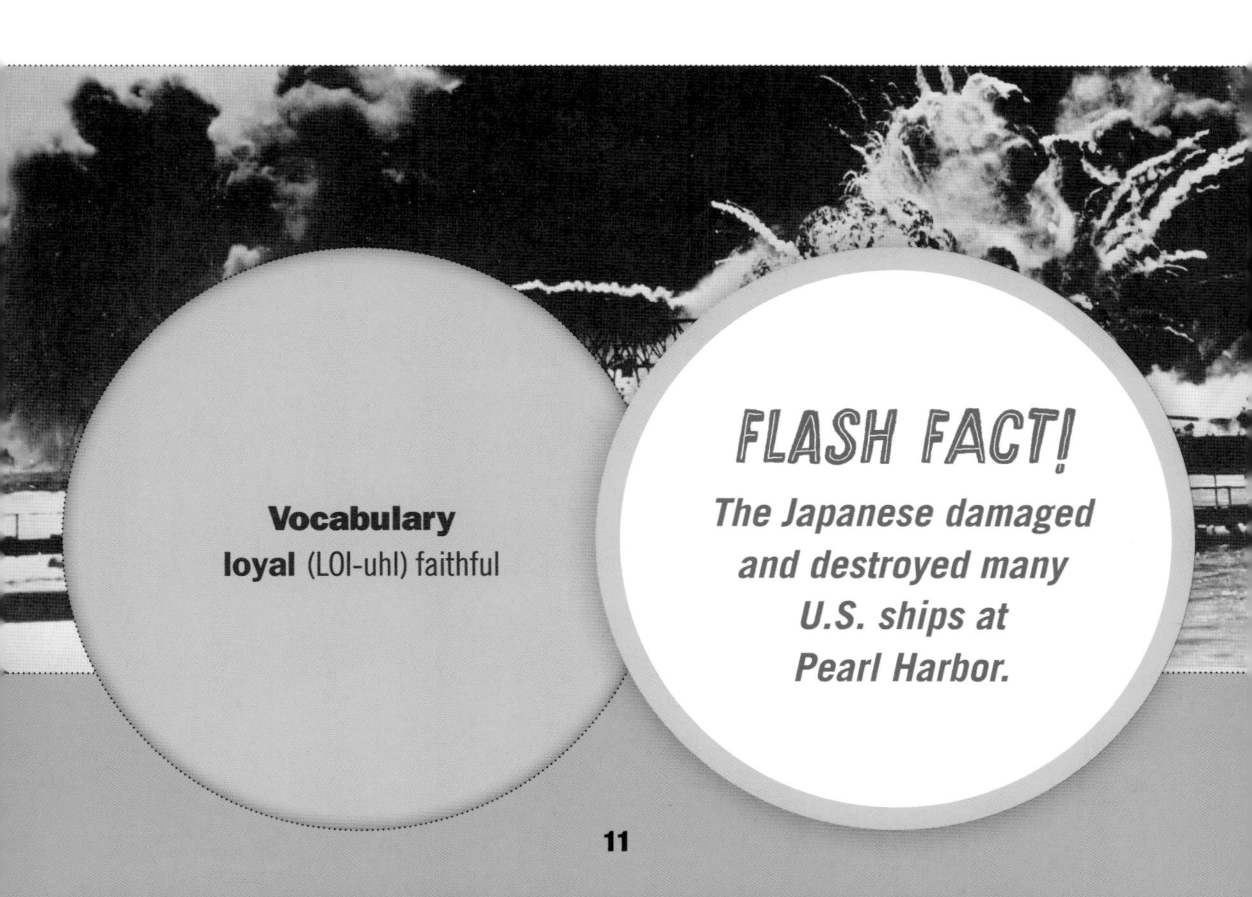

Vocabulary
loyal (LOI-uhl) faithful

FLASH FACT!
The Japanese damaged and destroyed many U.S. ships at Pearl Harbor.

NARRATOR: *The next day, the United States declared war on Japan. A few months later, the president signs Executive Order 9066.*

HELEN: Mother! Someone **slashed** our car's tires! I saw a sign that read "No Japs Wanted."

MRS. WATANABE: It doesn't matter now. Hurry! Grab as much as you can!

HELEN: Why? Where are we going?

MRS. WATANABE: We're being relocated. It's the law now.

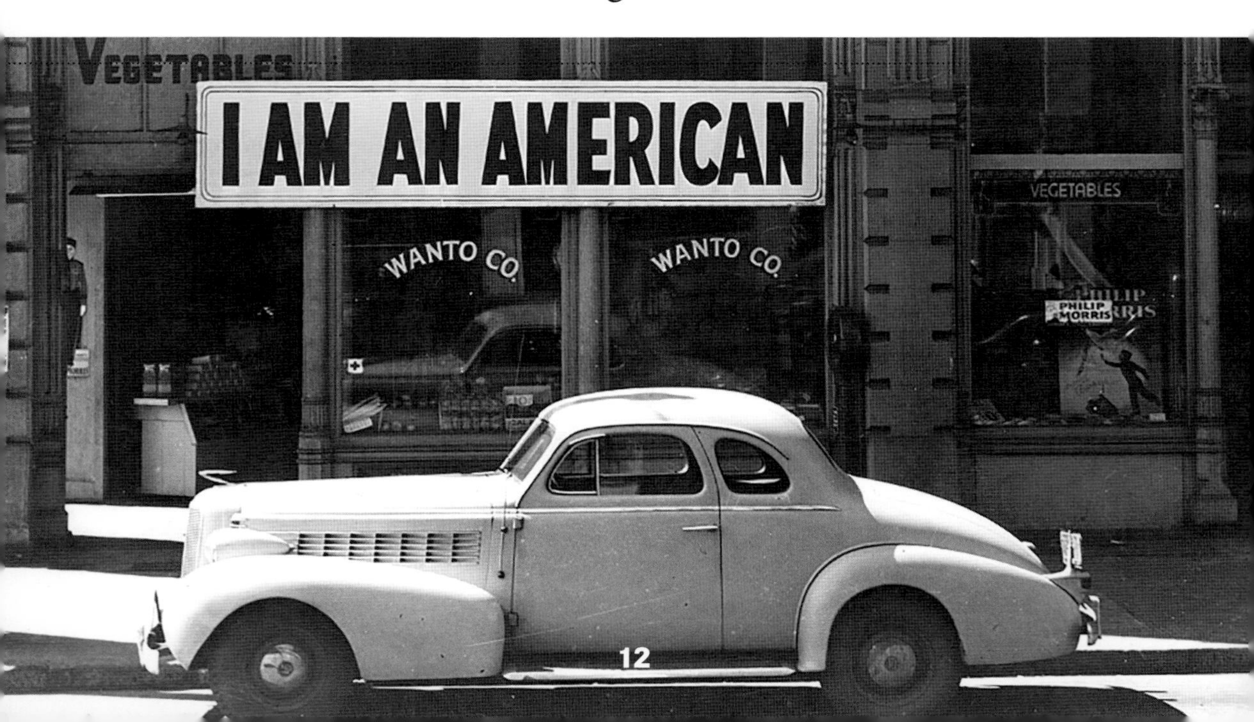

HELEN: Where will we go? This is our home.

MRS. WATANABE: We're getting a new home. We have to sell as much as we can. We'll have to leave everything else.

NARRATOR: *A* **SOLDIER** *knocks at the door.*

SOLDIER: Is this the Watanabe family?

HELEN: Yes.

SOLDIER: You need to start heading to the bus. We need to take you to the relocation center.

Vocabulary

slashed (SLASHD) to cut

FLASH FACT!

Many businesses would not serve Japanese customers.

HELEN: I just need to find my dog. His name is Max.

SOLDIER: You can't bring pets.

HELEN: I can't leave Max. He's part of the family.

SOLDIER: I don't have time for this. You need to go now.

MRS. WATANABE: Helen, it'll be okay. We're **survivors**. *Shikata ga nai.*

SOLDIER: What did you just say in Japanese? Are you spies?

HELEN: We're not spies. She just said, "It cannot be helped."

SOLDIER: I'll have to report this.

NARRATOR: *The Watanabe family is taken to a relocation center. There,* **HELEN WATANABE** *meets* **MAS YUBU***.*

LOCATION SHOOTING

REAL-WORLD SETTING

The Manzanar War Relocation Center was 1 of 10 Japanese internment camps. It's located in the Owens Valley of California. It's between the Sierra Nevada mountains on the west and the Inyo mountains on the east. It's desert land. The weather is harsh. The summers are really hot. The winters are below freezing. There are strong winds all year long. Dust and sand cover the camp. People would wake up covered in dust. They had to stay in shacks. They had no privacy. There were no doors in the bathrooms. The camp was surrounded by barbed wire and 8 guard towers. *Manzanar* means "apple orchard" in Spanish. Before it was a camp, it was a ranch. It grew peach, pear, and apple trees. Today, it's a national historic site. It's a museum. It's the most intact of all the camps.

Vocabulary

survivors (sur-VYE-vurz) people who live through a tough time

FLASH FACT!

The Japanese American Citizens League (JACL) is a group that works to protect the rights of Japanese Americans.

MAS: Are you lost?

HELEN: My mother told me to wait here. She's looking for my father. There are so many people here. We got separated. Did you get relocated too?

MAS: Yes. I was going to school at UCLA. A soldier came to my **dorm** room. He told me I had to leave. He said my father was taken to jail. I'm here to meet my family. I have to take care of them now.

HELEN: Why was he taken?

Vocabulary

dorm (DORM) a building at a college with many small rooms for sleeping

suspicious (suh-SPISH-uhs) not trustworthy

security (sih-KYOOR-ih-tee) safety

FLASH FACT!

Many people learned about the attack on Pearl Harbor from newspapers and radio.

MAS: My father is a community leader. Because of the war with Japan, all Japanese American leaders and teachers are **suspicious**. They think we're threats to national **security**. None of this makes sense.

HELEN: Why are they doing this to us?

MAS: People are scared. They're acting out of fear. But it's not fair. We're also at war with Italy and Germany. But only Japanese Americans are being interned.

NARRATOR: *A* **SOLDIER** *approaches.*

SOLDIER: Both of you stop **conspiring**. Move along. It's time to go to Manzanar.

NARRATOR: **GRACE JONES** *is at the relocation center. She's about to get on the bus when she is stopped by a* **SOLDIER**.

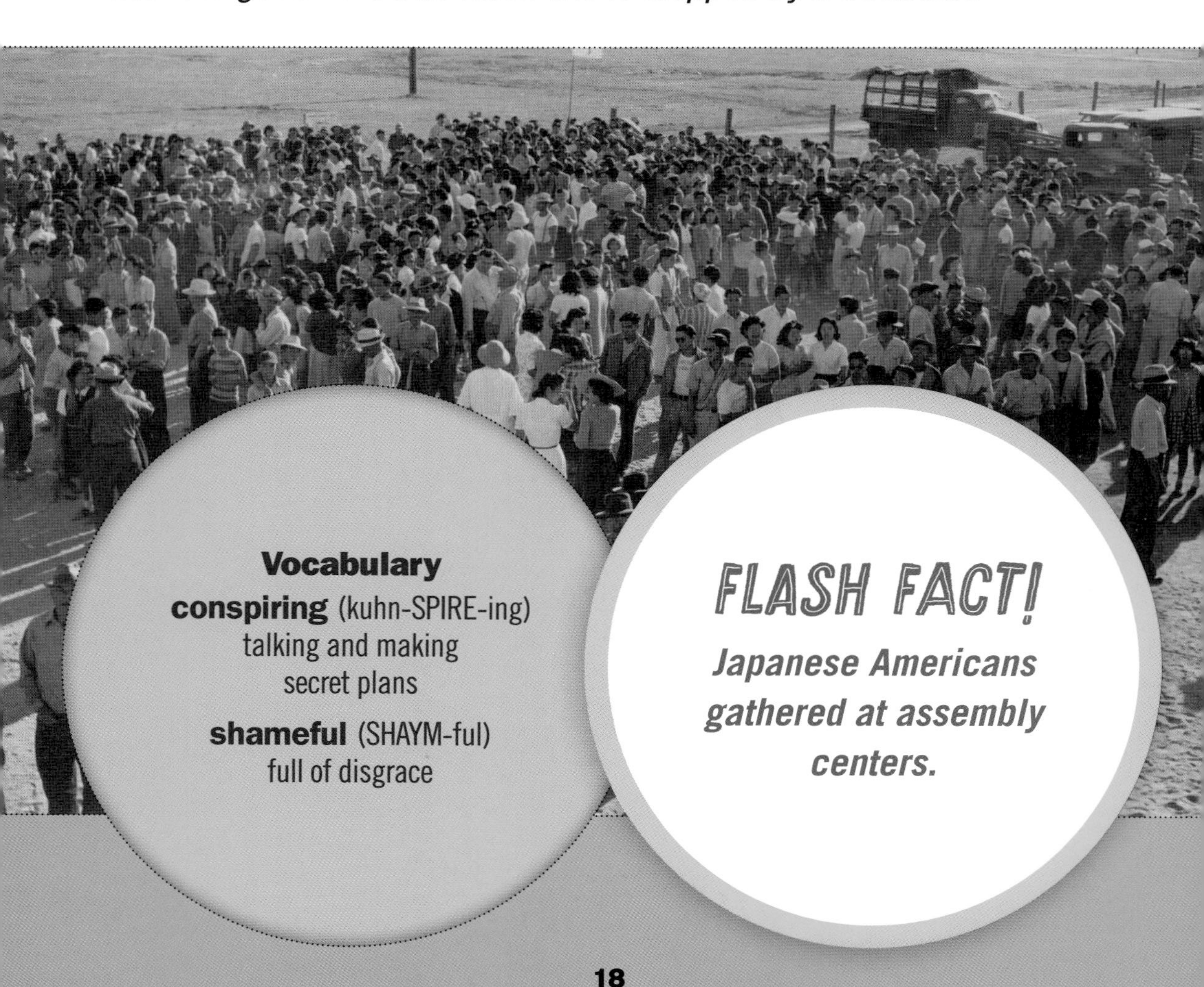

Vocabulary

conspiring (kuhn-SPIRE-ing)
talking and making secret plans

shameful (SHAYM-ful)
full of disgrace

FLASH FACT!

Japanese Americans gathered at assembly centers.

SOLDIER: What are you doing here? You're not Japanese.

GRACE: We're all Americans. It's **shameful** what you're doing here.

SOLDIER: I'm just doing my job. Please answer the question.

GRACE: Well, I'm doing my job as well. I work for the WRA. I've been assigned to Manzanar.

SOLDIER: What will you be doing there?

GRACE: I'm a teacher. I will be teaching.

SOLDIER: You couldn't get a teaching job somewhere else?

GRACE: Because of the war, there aren't many jobs. To my surprise, I was hired pretty quickly for this one.

SOLDIER: That's because no one wants to go to Manzanar.

NARRATOR: *Everyone arrives at Manzanar.* **HELEN WATANABE** *and* **MRS. WATANABE** *are waiting for instructions from a* **GUARD***.*

GUARD: You are now number 35456. You will stay at block 10, **barrack** 9, room 3.

MRS. WATANABE: What does that mean?

GUARD: These are blocks of houses. There are 36 blocks. Each block has 14 barracks. Each barrack has several rooms. Just look for your numbers.

HELEN: Mother, are we still in California? This doesn't look like Los Angeles.

MRS. WATANABE: It's the desert.

HELEN: Why are there all these men with guns here?

MRS. WATANABE: They're guards. See those fences. See those guard towers. They're all around us. This means we can't leave.

HELEN: It feels like jail.

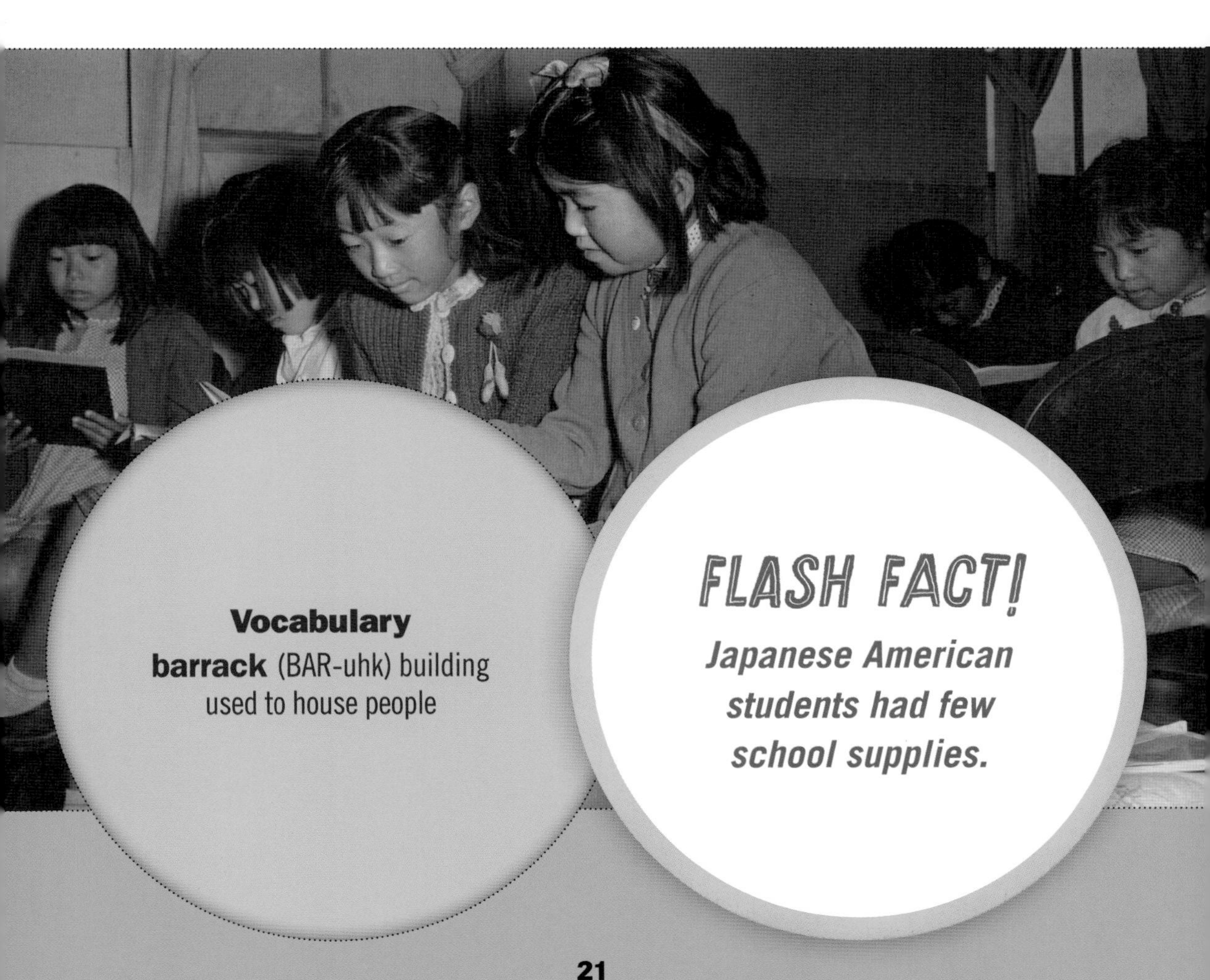

Vocabulary

barrack (BAR-uhk) building used to house people

FLASH FACT!

Japanese American students had few school supplies.

MRS. WATANABE: It's our life now.

HELEN: We only have one light bulb. We have one tiny stove. We have **cots**. The mattresses are stuffed with straw.

MRS. WATANABE: The worst part will be space. We have to share this room with another family. We also have to share the bathrooms with everyone in our barrack.

HELEN: What if I have to use the bathroom at night?

MRS. WATANABE: Don't go by yourself. You'll have to wake me up.

HELEN: I don't like it here. I want to go home.

NARRATOR: *Years have passed.* **HELEN WATANABE** *goes to school. She's talking to* **GRACE JONES**.

GRACE: Helen, why didn't you do your homework?

HELEN: It's hard to work at home. We don't have much space. It's very loud. Also, we don't have good light.

Vocabulary
cots (KAHTS) small beds

FLASH FACT!
Families had to share apartments with only 1 room.

GRACE: I see. Are you okay? How are things going?

HELEN: It was hard at first. But things are better. I help my parents with our gardens.

GRACE: You're gardening?

HELEN: The food here is not very good. We're used to eating rice and vegetables. So, we grow our own food.

GRACE: That's nice.

Vocabulary

glee (GLEE) a group that sings short songs

donations (doh-NAY-shuhnz) gifts

FLASH FACT!

At Manzanar, students walked from their barracks to their classrooms.

HELEN: I try to keep busy. I like school. I like my new friends. We sing in **glee** club. We take art classes. We're trying to make life better.

GRACE: Things are getting better. We finally got some **donations**. We bought desks and chairs so you don't have to sit on the floor anymore. We bought some books.

HELEN: I have to go. My friend Mas is playing in a baseball game. I haven't seen him in a long time. Come if you like!

NARRATOR: **MAS YUBU** *became a soldier in the U.S. Army. He comes back to Manzanar after his* ***tour of duty****. He sees* **HELEN WATANABE***.*

HELEN: That was a great game. You played well.

MAS: Thanks. It's so nice to see you again.

HELEN: How was the war?

MAS: I trained for 10 months. I fought battles in Italy and France. I helped rescue other soldiers. I served my country well. And then they sent me back here.

HELEN: That doesn't seem right at all. You risked your life. You proved your loyalty.

BLOOPERS

HISTORICAL MISTAKES

Executive Order 9066 was a big mistake. Experts today say it was a violation of human rights. Eleanor Roosevelt was President Franklin D. Roosevelt's wife. In April 1943, she visited the internment camp at the Gila River. The camp was in Arizona. She wanted to help the Japanese Americans. She thought the camps should be closed down at once. She didn't like what was happening. But she had to support her husband. Mrs. Roosevelt made a speech. She said, "To undo a mistake is always harder than not to create one originally." She also said, "We cannot progress if we look down upon any group of people amongst us because of race or religion. Every citizen in this country has a right to our basic freedoms, to justice and to equality of opportunity." This was her most public comment against her husband.

Vocabulary

tour of duty (TOOR UHV DOO-tee)
a period of time spent in combat

FLASH FACT!

The 442nd Regimental Combat Team is a military group of Japanese Americans. They fought on America's side in World War II.

MAS: Yes. But I still look Japanese.

HELEN: It's not fair what they're doing to us. That's why some of the men **rioted**.

MAS: What happened?

HELEN: Some guards beat up one of our leaders. There were angry mobs of people. Things got out of control.

MAS: That doesn't sound good.

HELEN: I can't wait to get out of here. Then we'll be free again.

MAS: We'll never really be free because we look different. We'll always have to fight for our freedom.

HELEN: I hope that this never happens to another group again.

Vocabulary

rioted (RYE-uht-id) disturbed the peace in a violent way

FLASH FACT!

People played and watched baseball at Manzanar. It was a way to pass the time.

EVENT TIMELINE

- **December 7, 1941: Japanese planes attack Pearl Harbor, in Honolulu, Hawaii.**
- **December 8, 1941: The United States enters World War II.**
- **February 19, 1942: President Franklin D. Roosevelt signs Executive Order 9066. This allows the military to relocate people thought to be enemies. It mainly applies to Japanese Americans.**
- **February 25, 1942: The U.S. Navy removes Japanese Americans living in Terminal Island near Los Angeles, California. They are given 48 hours to leave. This is the first group to be removed.**
- **February 27, 1942: Chase Clark is governor of Idaho. He said he'd take Japanese Americans if they were in camps under military guard. This may have inspired the idea of internment camps.**
- **March 18, 1942: The War Relocation Authority is established. Milton Eisenhower is the director. He later resigns. He doesn't agree with Executive Order 9066.**
- **March 24, 1942: The U.S. Army issues the first order to evacuate. It affects families in Bainbridge Island near Seattle, Washington. Japanese Americans are given one week to prepare to leave.**
- **June 2, 1942: All Japanese Americans in California, Oregon, Washington, and Arizona are relocated.**
- **February 1, 1943: The 442nd Regimental Combat Team is formed. It earns the most combat medals in American history.**
- **September 13, 1943: Tule Lake, in California, becomes a camp for people the government thinks are disloyal.**
- **December 17, 1944: Executive Order 9066 is revoked. Revoked means taken back.**
- **September 2, 1945: Japan surrenders. World War II is over.**
- **December 1945: All camps except Tule Lake are closed.**
- **March 1946: Tule Lake camp closes.**
- **August 10, 1988: The Civil Liberties Act of 1988 is passed by Congress. It's signed by President Ronald Reagan. The act apologizes for internment. It gives money to survivors.**

CONSIDER THIS!

TAKE A POSITION! What do you think about the Japanese internment camps? Were they fair or not? Should President Roosevelt have signed Executive Order 9066? Why or why not? Consider the time period. Argue your point with reasons and evidence.

SAY WHAT? Learn more about the Japanese internment camps. Explain how the Japanese Americans made a life at the camps. Describe how they lived. Describe what they did each day. Describe what they ate.

THINK ABOUT IT! Compare the Japanese internment camps to what is happening today. Learn more about immigration detention centers around the world. How are they like the Japanese internment camps? How are they different?

Learn More

Bailey, Rachel A. *The Japanese Internment Camps.* Ann Arbor, MI: Cherry Lake Publishing, 2014.

Sullivan, Laura L. *Life as a Child in a Japanese Internment Camp.* New York, NY: Cavendish Square, 2017.

Warren, Andrea. *Enemy Child: The Story of Norman Mineta, a Boy Imprisoned in a Japanese American Internment Camp during World War II.* New York, NY: Holiday House, 2019.

INDEX

Army, U.S., 26
assembly centers, 18

baseball, 29

Civil Liberties Act of 1988, 30

discrimination, 9

Executive Order 9066, 4, 12, 27, 30

Farewell to Manzanar, 9

Gila River internment camp, 27

Houston, Jeanne Wakatsuki, 9
human rights, 27

internment camps
See also Manzanar War Relocation Center
historical background, 4
life at, 9, 15, 18–26, 20–26
timeline, 30
U.S. apologizes for, 30
where they were, 7, 15

Japan, 4, 5, 10, 11
Japanese American Citizens League (JACL), 15
Japanese Americans, 4, 11, 13, 15
face prejudice and discrimination, 9
gathered at assembly centers, 18
seen as threat to national security, 17
sent to internment camps, 7
as soldiers, 26, 27, 28, 30
timeline, 30
Jones, Grace, 8, 18–19, 23–25

Manzanar War Relocation Center, 8, 9, 15
See also internment camps
baseball, 29
life at, 9, 20–26
school at, 21, 23–25

national security, 17

Pearl Harbor, 4, 5, 10, 11, 16, 30
prejudice, 9

relocation centers, 13, 14, 15, 30
riots, 28
Roosevelt, Eleanor, 27
Roosevelt, Franklin D., 4, 6, 27, 30

school, 21, 23–25
soldiers, Japanese Americans, 26, 27, 28, 30
spies, 4, 14

timeline, 30
Tule Lake camp, 30

War Relocation Authority (WRA), 4, 19, 30
Watanabe family, 8, 10–14, 16–17, 20–26
World War II, 4, 30

Yubu, Mas, 8, 14, 16–17, 26, 28

ABOUT THE AUTHOR

Dr. Virginia Loh-Hagan is an author, university professor, and former classroom teacher. She wants to tour all the internment camps in California. She lives in San Diego with her very tall husband and very naughty dogs. To learn more about her, visit www.virginialoh.com.